This Jo

_____

> "Making the decision to have a child is momentous. It is to decide forever to have your heart go walking around outside your body."
> Elizabeth Stone

This Journal is my gift to you, my child. It is a keepsake that I hope you will treasure forever.

My thoughts and emotions when I
first found out about the
pregnancy, who I told first, etc. .....

_____

_____

_____

_____

_____

_____

_____

_____

_____

_____

_____

What I looked like before you were born (add picture):

My age:

DOB:

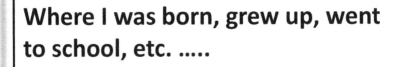

Where I was born, grew up, went to school, etc. .....

_____

_____

_____

_____

_____

_____

_____

_____

_____

_____

_____

"There are two lasting bequests we can give our children. One is roots. The other is wings." Hodding Carter Jr.

My hopes and dreams for you as you grow up include .....

_____

_____

_____

_____

_____

_____

_____

_____

_____

_____

_____

"It is a smile of a baby
that makes life worth
living."
Debasish Mridha

This is what I liked to do as a kid .....

When I was a kid, things I didn't like to do .....

_____

_____

_____

_____

_____

_____

_____

_____

_____

_____

_____

"The amazing thing about becoming a parent is that you will never again be your own first priority." Olivia Wilde

This is what I want you to know about your other family members .....

_____

_____

_____

_____

_____

_____

_____

_____

_____

_____

_____

What you have taught me about life so far .....

_____

_____

_____

_____

_____

_____

_____

_____

_____

_____

_____

_____

My earliest and best childhood memories include .....

_____

_____

_____

_____

_____

_____

_____

_____

_____

_____

_____

Your first breath took mine away.

Special skills I have include .....

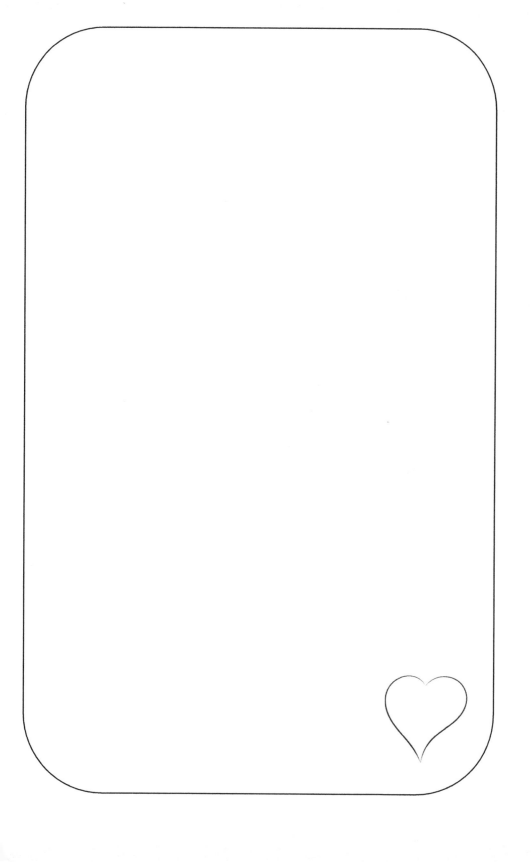

My first jobs, rate of pay, what I spent my money on .....

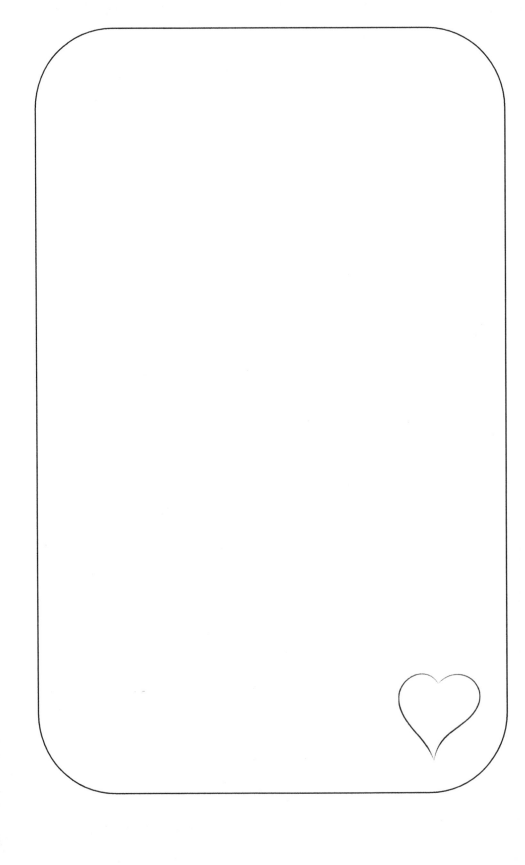

My best advice to you as you grow up .....

_____

_____

_____

_____

_____

_____

_____

_____

_____

_____

_____

_____

**Great things come in
small packages.**

My favorite music – songs, artists were/are .....

_____

_____

_____

_____

_____

_____

_____

_____

_____

_____

_____

_____

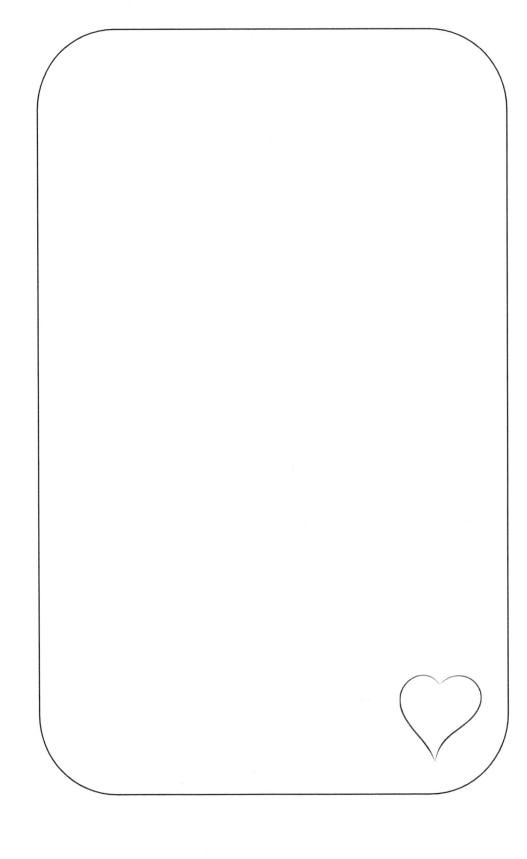

My favorite T.V. shows and movies were/are, because .....

_____

_____

_____

_____

_____

_____

_____

_____

_____

_____

_____

_____

"Children see magic
because they look for it."
Christopher Moore

No one is perfect. My strengths and weaknesses include ......and this is what I've done to adapt .....

_____

_____

_____

_____

_____

_____

_____

_____

_____

_____

_____

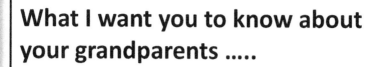

What I want you to know about your grandparents .....

_____

_____

_____

_____

_____

_____

_____

_____

_____

_____

_____

_____

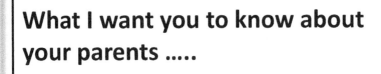

What I want you to know about your parents .....

_____

_____

_____

_____

_____

_____

_____

_____

_____

_____

_____

"A father is someone you can look up to, no matter how tall you grow."
Unknown author

Something that I learned the hard way was .....

_____

_____

_____

_____

_____

_____

_____

_____

_____

_____

_____

_____

What I did to prepare for your birth
.....

"Any man can be a
father, but it takes
someone special to be a
daddy." Anne Geddes

My favorite toys as a kid included .....

The best lessons that I have learned in life include .....

_____

_____

_____

_____

_____

_____

_____

_____

_____

_____

_____

Things that I am most proud about include .....

_____

_____

_____

_____

_____

_____

_____

_____

_____

_____

_____

_____

"My father gave me the greatest gift anyone could give another person, he believed in me."
Jim Valvano

My favorite vacations include .....

_____

_____

_____

_____

_____

_____

_____

_____

_____

_____

_____

_____

My memories of seeing you on ultrasound for the first time, hearing your heart beat, etc. .....

_____

_____

_____

_____

_____

_____

_____

_____

_____

_____

_____

_____

Baby names we considered, why and how we decided .....

"I cannot think of any need in childhood as strong as the need for a father's protection."
Sigmund Freud

My memory of the day you entered the world .....

_____

_____

_____

_____

_____

_____

_____

_____

_____

_____

_____

_____

People I find inspirational and the reasons why include .....

_____

_____

_____

_____

_____

_____

_____

_____

_____

_____

_____

My favorite memories of the pregnancy include .....

_____

_____

_____

_____

_____

_____

_____

_____

_____

_____

_____

_____

"My father used to say that it's never too late to do anything you wanted to do. And he said, 'You never know what you can accomplish until you try.'"
Michael Jordan

The most important things in life are and the reasons why .....

_____

_____

_____

_____

_____

_____

_____

_____

_____

_____

_____

_____

What I want to teach you and do with you as you grow up .....

_____

_____

_____

_____

_____

_____

_____

_____

_____

_____

_____

_____

_____

What I hope you will always remember about me .....

"While we try to teach
our children all about life,
our children teach us
what life is all about."
Angela Schwindt

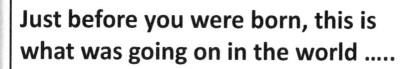

**Just before you were born, this is
what was going on in the world .....**

_____

_____

_____

_____

_____

_____

_____

_____

_____

_____

_____

_____

My favorite season, time of day, holiday destinations, things to say, etc. .....

_____

_____

_____

_____

_____

_____

_____

_____

_____

_____

_____

"If I could reach up and hold a star for everytime you've made me smile, the entire evening sky would be in the palm of my hand." Author unknown

My thoughts and emotions when I first met you .....

_____

_____

_____

_____

_____

_____

_____

_____

_____

_____

_____

This is my first love letter to you, my sweet child .....

"A child reaches for your hand, and touches your heart." Author unknown

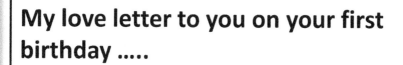

My love letter to you on your first birthday .....

"My father taught me not to overthink things, that nothing will ever be perfect, so just keep moving and do your best." Scott Eastwood

"Being a father has been, without a doubt, my greatest source of achievement, pride and inspiration. Fatherhood has taught me about unconditional love, reinforced the importance of giving back and taught me how to be a better person."

Naveen Jain

Made in the USA
Monee, IL
30 May 2020